The Bill of Rights

DAVID & PATRICIA ARMENTROUT

Rourke
Publishing LLC
Vero Beach, Florida 32964

DOCUMENTS THAT SHAPED THE NATION

www.rourkepublishing.com

PHOTO CREDITS: Pages 16, 18, 28, 29 © Getty Images. Pages 5, 11 © PhotoDisc, Inc. Pages 19, 21 from Images of Political History. Pages 32, 33 © Jupiter Images. Page 41 Courtesy of the LBJ Library and O. J. Rapp Pages 42, 43 Courtesy of the U.S. National Archives and Records Administration and Earl McDonald. All other images from the Library of Congress

Title page: *A 1963 civil rights march in Washington, D.C.*

Editor: Frank Sloan

Cover and page design by Nicola Stratford

Library of Congress Cataloging-in-Publication Data

Armentrout, David, 1962-
    The Bill of Rights / David and Patricia Armentrout.
        p. cm. -- (Documents that shaped the nation)
    Includes bibliographical references (p.   ) and index.
        ISBN 1-59515-234-2 (hardcover)   141 7967
    1. United States. Constitution. 1st-10th Amendments--Juvenile
literature.
    2. Constitutional amendments--United States--Juvenile literature. 3.
Civil
 rights--United States--Juvenile literature.   I. Armentrout, Patricia,
1960-   .
    II. Title.
    KF4750.A76 2004
    342.7308'5--dc22

2004014419

Printed in the USA
CG

TABLE OF CONTENTS

HUMAN RIGHTS

Most Americans take human rights and civil liberties for granted. Because we live in the United States, it could be easy to assume that people everywhere are treated with basic human rights and are protected by civil liberties. It can be shocking to learn that in some nations, people have very few, if any, guaranteed rights. Some nations have governments that rule by absolute power. The rights of their people are considered less important than the rights of the state, or government.

The United States has enemies, but most of the world's people admire and respect what the United States stands for. Given the opportunity to pick one word that describes the United States, many would say "freedom." The people of the United States are fortunate to have the protection of some of the most powerful documents ever written. The Charters of Freedom documents include the Declaration of Independence, the Constitution, and the Bill of Rights. Together, they serve as the foundation for government in the United

Civil liberties are rights and freedoms that are protected by law. Human rights are basic rights that should belong to everyone simply because they are human.

4

The Statue of Liberty on Liberty Island in New York Harbor

States. Together, the Charters of Freedom explain the **principles** by which our nation was founded and guarantee the freedoms we enjoy.

A CRY TO BE HEARD

In the early days of America, when Great Britain ruled the 13 American colonies, human rights were often overlooked. British **Parliament** passed laws that were in

the interest of Great Britain, without considering the best interests of the colonies. Colonists had very little, if any, power to eliminate or change these laws.

Time and time again, the colonists demanded basic rights from Great Britain. They pleaded with their mother country to allow them **representation** in British Parliament. When their requests were not heard, the colonists responded in the best way they knew how. They staged protests. They refused to buy British products. They wrote papers defending their cause and accusing British Parliament. The colonies even formed their own group of representatives, or Congress, to stand up for their rights.

Surely, their mother country would listen now. However, Great Britain underestimated the anger that was building in the colonies. Instead of listening to their concerns, Great Britain decided to use force to control the colonists. It was this decision that would alter the course of history.

Lord North was the British Prime Minister from 1770 to 1782. He was responsible for governing the American colonies.

DECLARING INDEPENDENCE

The American Revolution had already begun when the Second Continental Congress declared independence from Great Britain in 1776. The colonists had made their choice. They chose war over **tyranny**. They chose freedom!

With the signing of the Declaration of Independence, Congress set about the task of creating a workable government. The experience of having been ruled so harshly by Great Britain caused many colonists and members of Congress to fear powerful government. No one was willing to trade one bad government for another. A set of laws called a Constitution was needed to create a central government, but also to protect the independence of the states. The colonists wanted the powers of the government to be in writing, so everyone would know what those powers were.

Patrick Henry, a famous patriot and delegate to the Continental Congress, once said, "I know not what course others may take; but as for me, give me liberty or give me death!" Many colonists felt the same way.

Patrick Henry giving his famous speech

THE ARTICLES OF CONFEDERATION

The first national Constitution was known as the Articles of Confederation. It was **adopted** by Congress in 1777, but not fully **ratified** by all 13 states until 1781. It allowed for the creation of a central, or federal, government, but left most real power within the states. Once the Articles of Confederation had been ratified by all 13 states, Congress was given a new name, "The United States in Congress Assembled."

The states had also been working on their own Constitutions. In fact, all 13 states had ratified each state's Constitution by 1780, a year before the Articles of Confederation was fully ratified. Many of the state Constitutions also included a bill of rights to protect the rights of individuals.

The Articles of Confederation were adopted by Congress at Independence Hall in Philadelphia.

*The surrender of Lord Cornwallis and 8,000 British soldiers
at Yorktown brought about the end of the Revolutionary War.*

The American Revolution, or War of Independence as it is sometimes called, was long and bloody. Thousands died on both sides, but the American colonists would finish what they started. Although most of the fighting was over by the end of 1781, a treaty ending the war with Great Britain was not signed until 1783. The world now knew that the United States was free and independent. Success of the new nation, however, was not guaranteed. There was still much work to be done.

The Articles of Confederation proved to be a weak national Constitution. This document protected the independence of the states but left the federal government without strength. Congress was not able to make trade agreements with other nations or collect taxes directly from the people. The federal government could not operate properly because it had no authority to enforce rules or laws. The Articles of Confederation also offered little in the way of individual rights.

THE CONSTITUTIONAL CONVENTION

If the national government could not function, the very survival of the new nation would be in doubt. Congress agreed that changes, or amendments, to the Articles of Confederation were needed.

In May of 1787, delegates were sent to a special meeting in Philadelphia to discuss the issues. The historic meeting is now called the Constitutional Convention. Many of the delegates believed the problems with the Articles of Confederation could not be corrected. Rather

than attempting to fix the Articles as they had been instructed, the delegates began writing a completely new Constitution.

Delegates attending the Constitutional Convention often met and dined at City Tavern in Philadelphia.

George Washington was named
the president of the
Constitutional Convention.

A NEW CONSTITUTION

Convention delegates debated different plans that proposed a structure for the new Constitution. The Virginia Plan, written by James Madison, quickly became the favorite. Madison's plan suggested a national government consisting of three branches. A Legislative branch made up of two houses would make the laws. An Executive branch headed by the president would enforce the laws. The Judicial branch would explain and interpret the laws when there was disagreement. The three branches of government insured that there would be a system of *checks and balances* to prevent the abuse of power.

Although Madison's plan was favored, there were disagreements. One of the disagreements was about the number of representatives each state would be allowed. Larger states felt they should have more representatives because they had more people. States with smaller populations did not want to allow larger states to have too much power. In what is now called the Great **Compromise**, the delegates agreed to changes that satisfied the concerns of both. The Constitution is full of compromises, some small, some large. A compromise means you get less than you want. Without compromise, however, the delegates would not have been able to finish the Constitution.

James Madison is sometimes called the Father of our Constitution. James Madison went on to become the fourth president of the United States.

George Washington addresses convention delegates.

NO BILL OF RIGHTS?

In 1787, after four months of hard work, the delegates had prepared a final draft of the new Constitution. All but three of the delegates present signed the finished work. One of the biggest opponents of the new constitution was George Mason, a delegate from Virginia. Strangely enough, Mason had been very helpful in its creation.

George Mason refused to sign the Constitution.

Elbridge Gerry believed the new Constitution gave the federal government too much control over the states.

Mason was not as upset about what was in the Constitution as he was about what was not in the Constitution. Mason argued passionately that the Constitution needed to guarantee more individual rights. The Constitution, Mason said, needed a bill of rights. Mason would not give his approval of the Constitution without one.

George Mason also disagreed with a provision in the Constitution that would allow slavery to continue until 1808. Mason believed that all men should be free and that slavery should be abolished. Mason felt this way despite the fact that he was a slave owner himself.

Edmund Randolph, George Mason, and Elbridge Gerry were the only three delegates present at the Constitutional Convention who refused to sign the Constitution.

RATIFICATION OF THE CONSTITUTION

The signed Constitution was sent to Congress. Congress reviewed the document before sending it to the states where it would begin the ratification process. The Constitution required 9 of the 13 states to ratify it. This was done by June of 1788, which allowed Congress to replace the Articles of Confederation with the new Constitution. By 1790 all 13 states had ratified the Constitution.

There was still widespread distrust of the new Constitution. It was an improvement over the Articles of Confederation, but it increased the power of the federal government without protecting civil liberties. The states did ratify the Constitution as it was written, but many did so with the understanding that a *bill of rights* would soon be added. In fact, six of the states attached a list of proposed amendments to their approval.

The final wording of the Constitution and the style with which it is written is credited to a delegate from Pennsylvania named Gouverneur Morris.

The delegate from Pennsylvania, Gouverneur Morris

THE BILL OF RIGHTS IS APPROVED

D. Watson's.

BILL OF RIGHTS.

A Declaration of Rights made by the Representatives of the good People of VIRGINIA, *assembled in full and free Convention; which rights do pertain to them, and their Posterity, as the basis and foundation of Government.*

[Unanimously adopted, June 12th, 1776.]

1. That all men are by nature equally free and independent, and have certain inherent rights, of which, when they enter into a state of society, they cannot, by any compact, deprive or divest their posterity; namely, the enjoyment of life and liberty, with the means of acquiring and possessing property, and pursuing and obtaining happiness and safety.

2. That all power is vested in, and consequently derived from, the people; that Magistrates are their trustees and servants, and at all times amenable to them.

3. That government is, or ought to be, instituted for the common benefit, protection and security of the people, nation, or community: of all the various modes and forms of government, that is best, which is capable of producing the greatest degree of happiness and safety, and is most effectually secured against the danger of mal-administration; and that, when any government shall be found inadequate or contrary to these purposes, a majority of the community hath an indubitable, unalienable, and indefeasible right, to reform, alter, or abolish it, in such manner as shall be judged most conducive to the public weal.

4. That no man, or set of men, are entitled to exclusive or separate emoluments or privileges from the community, but in consideration of public services; which not being descendible, neither ought the offices of Magistrate, Legislator, or Judge, to be hereditary.

5. That the Legislative and Executive powers of the State should be separate and distinct from the Judiciary; and that the members of the two first may be restrained from oppression, by feeling and participating the burthens of the people, they should, at fixed periods, be reduced to a private station, return into that body from which they were originally taken, and the vacancies be supplied by frequent, certain, and regular elections, in which all, or any part of the former members, to be again eligible, or ineligible, as the laws shall direct.

6. That elections of members to serve as representatives of the people, in Assembly, ought to be free; and that all men, having sufficient evidence of permanent common interest with, and attach-

The Virginia Declaration of Rights written by George Mason.

George Mason had been right all along, and many in Congress knew it. The people wanted and needed the protection of a bill of rights.

The first Congress, set up under the new Constitution, could not ignore the call for a bill of rights. James Madison led the way. In 1789, Madison proposed amending the Constitution. The amendments Madison proposed were modeled after the Virginia Declaration of Rights written by none other than George Mason.

Congress debated and changed many of the amendments, finally agreeing to submit them to the states for ratification. Ten of the twelve amendments were eventually approved by the states. The first ten amendments are now known as the Bill of Rights. On December 15, 1791, the amendments became a permanent addition to the United States Constitution.

James Madison served two terms as president of the United States.

In 1941, President Franklin Roosevelt declared December 15 as Bill of Rights day. In 2002, President George W. Bush declared December 10 as Human Rights Day.

THE PREAMBLE TO
THE BILL OF RIGHTS

The beautiful, but formal, wording used by the founding fathers to write the Charters of Freedom can be difficult to understand. The introduction, or preamble, to the bill of rights explains that the states wanted amendments added to the Constitution protecting its citizens from the abuse of power.

The Bill of Rights was written by the First Congress at Federal Hall in New York City. At that time, New York City was the nation's capital. The capital was moved to Philadelphia in 1790.

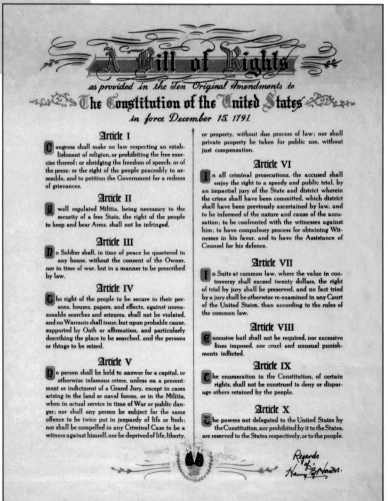

A Bill of Rights

as provided in the Ten Original Amendments to

The Constitution of the United States

in force December 15, 1791.

Article I

Congress shall make no law respecting an establishment of religion, or prohibiting the free exercise thereof; or abridging the freedom of speech, or of the press; or the right of the people peaceably to assemble, and to petition the Government for a redress of grievances.

Article II

A well regulated Militia, being necessary to the security of a free State, the right of the people to keep and bear Arms, shall not be infringed.

Article III

No Soldier shall, in time of peace be quartered in any house, without the consent of the Owner, nor in time of war, but in a manner to be prescribed by law.

Article IV

The right of the people to be secure in their persons, houses, papers, and effects, against unreasonable searches and seizures, shall not be violated, and no Warrants shall issue, but upon probable cause, supported by Oath or affirmation, and particularly describing the place to be searched, and the persons or things to be seized.

Article V

No person shall be held to answer for a capital, or otherwise infamous crime, unless on a presentment or indictment of a Grand Jury, except in cases arising in the land or naval forces, or in the Militia, when in actual service in time of War or public danger; nor shall any person be subject for the same offence to be twice put in jeopardy of life or limb; nor shall be compelled in any Criminal Case to be a witness against himself, nor be deprived of life, liberty, or property, without due process of law; nor shall private property be taken for public use, without just compensation.

Article VI

In all criminal prosecutions, the accused shall enjoy the right to a speedy and public trial, by an impartial jury of the State and district wherein the crime shall have been committed, which district shall have been previously ascertained by law, and to be informed of the nature and cause of the accusation; to be confronted with the witnesses against him; to have compulsory process for obtaining Witnesses in his favor, and to have the Assistance of Counsel for his defence.

Article VII

In Suits at common law, where the value in controversy shall exceed twenty dollars, the right of trial by jury shall be preserved, and no fact tried by a jury shall be otherwise re-examined in any Court of the United States, than according to the rules of the common law.

Article VIII

Excessive bail shall not be required, nor excessive fines imposed, nor cruel and unusual punishments inflicted.

Article IX

The enumeration in the Constitution, of certain rights, shall not be construed to deny or disparage others retained by the people.

Article X

The powers not delegated to the United States by the Constitution, nor prohibited by it to the States, are reserved to the States respectively, or to the people.

Regards of
Harry B Davis

Congress of the United States

begun and held at the City of New-York, on Wednesday the fourth of March, one thousand seven hundred and eighty nine.

The Conventions of a number of the States, having at the time of their adopting the Constitution, expressed a desire, in order to prevent misconstruction or abuse of its powers, that further declaratory and restrictive clauses should be added: And as extending the ground of public confidence in the Government, will best ensure the beneficent ends of its institution.

Resolved by the Senate and House of Representatives of the United States of America, in Congress assembled, two thirds of both Houses concurring, that the following Articles be proposed to the Legislatures of the several States, as amendments to the Constitution of the United States, all, or any of which Articles, when ratified by three fourths of the said Legislatures, to be valid to all intents and purposes, as part of the said Constitution.

ARTICLES in addition to, and Amendment of the Constitution of the United States of America, proposed by Congress, and ratified by the Legislatures of the several States, pursuant to the fifth Article of the original Constitution.

The Bill of Rights includes the first ten amendments to the Constitution.

THE FIRST TEN AMENDMENTS

The first amendment protects freedom of religion, freedom of speech, and freedom of the press. As with all freedoms, there are limits. For example, you have the right to voice your opinion, but do you have the right to make false statements that could harm others? The limits to our freedoms are constantly being tested.

Amendment I

Congress shall make no law respecting an establishment of religion, or prohibiting the free exercise thereof; or abridging the freedom of speech, or of the press; or the right of the people peaceably to assemble, and to petition the government for a redress of grievances.

The meaning behind the second amendment is often debated. Some believe it gives individuals the right to own and carry firearms. Others believe it simply protects the rights of states to maintain **militias**.

Amendment II

A well regulated militia, being necessary to the security of a free state, the right of the people to keep and bear arms, shall not be infringed.

The first amendment allows citizens to demonstrate peacefully.

Police can search a suspect if they have reason to suspect criminal activity.

The third amendment protects citizens from being forced to house soldiers. This amendment may have been an issue for colonists, but is not typically important in the modern world.

Amendment III
No soldier shall, in time of peace be quartered in any house, without the consent of the owner, nor in time of war, but in a manner to be prescribed by law.

The fourth amendment prohibits law enforcement officials from searching people or their homes and other possessions without reasonable cause and/or a legal **warrant**.

Amendment IV

The right of the people to be secure in their persons, houses, papers, and effects, against unreasonable searches and seizures, shall not be violated, and no warrants shall issue, but upon probable cause, supported by oath or affirmation, and particularly describing the place to be searched, and the persons or things to be seized.

Police cannot search private property without a search warrant or good cause.

The fifth amendment prohibits citizens from being found guilty of a crime without legal process. The fifth amendment also protects individuals from being forced to make statements that would prove them guilty of a criminal offense. In other words, those who have been charged with a crime have the right to remain silent.

Amendment V

No person shall be held to answer for a capital, or otherwise infamous crime, unless on a presentment or indictment of a grand jury, except in cases arising in the land or naval forces, or in the militia, when in actual service in time of war or public danger; nor shall any person be subject for the same offense to be twice put in jeopardy of life or limb; nor shall be compelled in any criminal case to be a witness against himself, nor be deprived of life, liberty, or property, without due process of law; nor shall private property be taken for public use, without just compensation.

The Bill of Rights gives citizens the right to be defended by a lawyer. A lawyer defends his client in court.

The sixth amendment protects the rights of the accused to a quick and fair trial and gives them the right to be defended by a lawyer.

Amendment VI

In all criminal prosecutions, the accused shall enjoy the right to a speedy and public trial, by an impartial jury of the state and district wherein the crime shall have been committed, which district shall have been previously ascertained by law, and to be informed of the nature and cause of the accusation; to be confronted with the witnesses against him; to have compulsory process for obtaining witnesses in his favor, and to have the assistance of counsel for his defense.

The seventh amendment gives the accused the right to be judged by a **jury**. The seventh amendment also prohibits an individual from being tried for the same crime twice.

Amendment VII

In suits at common law, where the value in controversy shall exceed twenty dollars, the right of trial by jury shall be preserved, and no fact tried by a jury, shall be otherwise reexamined in any court of the United States, than according to the rules of the common law.

The legal system in the United States follows the laws established by the Constitution.

The eighth amendment protects individuals found guilty of a crime from cruel and unusual punishments.

Amendment VIII

Excessive bail shall not be required, nor excessive fines imposed, nor cruel and unusual punishments inflicted.

A jury is a group of people that listen to a legal trial and then decide if the accused is innocent or guilty.

The ninth amendment states that the Constitution cannot deny other rights.

Amendment IX

The enumeration in the Constitution, of certain rights, shall not be construed to deny or disparage others retained by
the people.

The tenth amendment states that any powers not specifically mentioned in the Constitution remain under the control of the state or people.

Amendment X

The powers not delegated to the United States by the Constitution, nor prohibited by it to the states, are reserved to the states respectively, or to the people.

Women march in a parade demanding the right to vote. Women did not receive voting rights until the nineteenth amendment was added to the Constitution in 1920.

OTHER IMPORTANT AMENDMENTS

The Bill of Rights, ratified in 1791, guaranteed many of the freedoms Americans still enjoy. But the Bill of Rights did not originally apply to everyone equally. Though freedom was the basis for many of our founding documents, slavery remained legal in parts of the United States for many years. The issue of slavery was one of the main causes of the Civil War, the bloodiest war ever fought on American soil. Black Americans were not specifically guaranteed freedom until the thirteenth amendment abolished slavery in 1865.

The fourteenth amendment, ratified in 1868, was intended to prevent state governments from reducing the rights of former slaves. Since then, however, courts have used it to prevent states from reducing any of the liberties granted to individuals under the Bill of Rights.

Some Constitutional amendments were added to provide additional rights to individuals. Some were added to change the workings of the government. In one case, the eighteenth amendment, ratified in 1919, made the manufacture or sale of alcoholic drinks illegal (prohibition). It was then repealed, or canceled, in 1933 by the twenty-first amendment.

Some states passed their own laws against slavery including this Missouri proclamation signed just weeks before the thirteenth amendment was ratified.

Huge strides have been made in protecting the liberties of all people since the signing of the Bill of Rights. Civil liberties for **minorities** and women, however, were slow in

PUBLISHED & PRINTED BY — Entered according to act of Congress in the year 1870 by Th. Kelly in the Office of the Librarian of Congress at Washington D.C. — TH

THE FIFTEENTH AMENDMENT

coming. In 1870, the fifteenth amendment was ratified. It states that a person cannot be denied the right to vote based on their race or color. Finally, in 1920, the nineteenth amendment was ratified guaranteeing the right of women to vote.

In all, 27 amendments have been added to the Constitution. Others have been proposed, but not ratified. Many amendments were designed to guarantee basic rights, but discrimination based on race and/or sex has been difficult to eliminate.

A 1913 parade in Washington, D.C., in support of women's rights.

A celebration of the passing of the fifteenth amendment

CIVIL LIBERTIES FOR ALL

President Lyndon B. Johnson signed the Civil Rights Act of 1964. The Act strengthened laws against racial discrimination in public places. Other civil rights laws were passed in 1957, 1960, 1965, and most recently in 1991. The new laws are intended to fill in gaps left by the Constitution.

Our Constitution and its amendments were written to protect civil rights. The laws are strong. Sometimes, they can have the unintended effect of protecting criminals from punishment. For example, in 1963, Ernesto Miranda kidnapped and abused an 18-year-old girl. Miranda confessed to the crime, was found guilty in a court of law, and sentenced to prison.

The Miranda Warning:
You have the right to remain silent. Anything you say can and will be used against you in a court of law. You have the right to speak to an attorney, and to have an attorney present during any questioning. If you cannot afford a lawyer, one will be provided for you at government expense.

In 1966, Miranda's lawyers appealed the decision to the Supreme Court. His lawyers claimed that Miranda had not been told of his Fifth Amendment right to remain silent. The United States Supreme Court heard the case and agreed. Miranda was set free. Since then, police routinely recite the Miranda Warning before questioning a suspect.

President Lyndon B. Johnson signing the Civil Rights Act of 1964

PRESERVING THE DOCUMENT

The Charters of Freedom may be the most important collection of political documents in the world. Unfortunately, the documents were not always stored under the best conditions. Exposure to sunlight and moisture has caused the documents to deteriorate.

Extra care is taken to prevent further damage of the historic documents.

In the early 1950s, scientists came up with a plan to protect the documents. The documents were preserved in sealed cases protected from the environment by the best technology available at the time. Even under these conditions, the Charters of Freedom were not completely safe. Careful monitoring of the documents and their encasements showed very small changes that could damage the documents.

A cut-away view of a new encasement designed to protect the Charters of Freedom.

In July 2001, the Bill of Rights, the Declaration of Independence, and the Constitution were removed from display as part of a major restoration project. Scientists carefully removed the documents from the cases that had protected them for 50 years. Using microscopes, they examined every detail of each **parchment**. Small repairs were made where necessary and each parchment was cleaned and restored. New cases, built using the latest preservation technology, were then installed. Finally, the documents were sealed in their new protective environments ready for display. The Charters of Freedom were put back on public display at the National Archives in Washington, D.C., in September of 2003.

TIME LINE

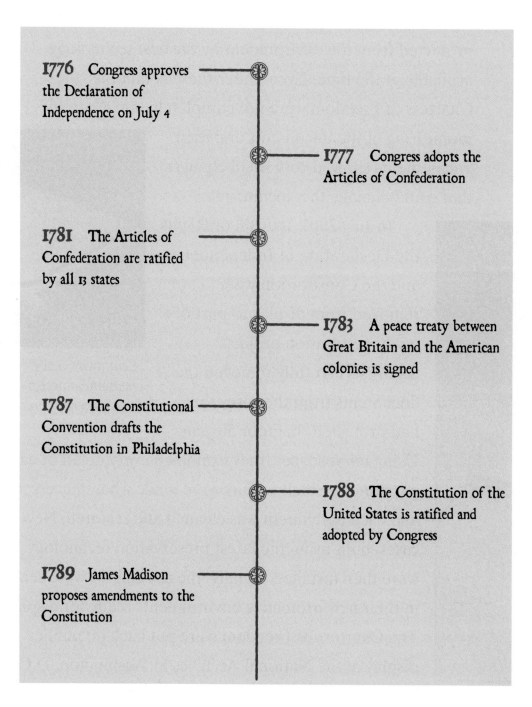

1776 Congress approves the Declaration of Independence on July 4

1777 Congress adopts the Articles of Confederation

1781 The Articles of Confederation are ratified by all 13 states

1783 A peace treaty between Great Britain and the American colonies is signed

1787 The Constitutional Convention drafts the Constitution in Philadelphia

1788 The Constitution of the United States is ratified and adopted by Congress

1789 James Madison proposes amendments to the Constitution

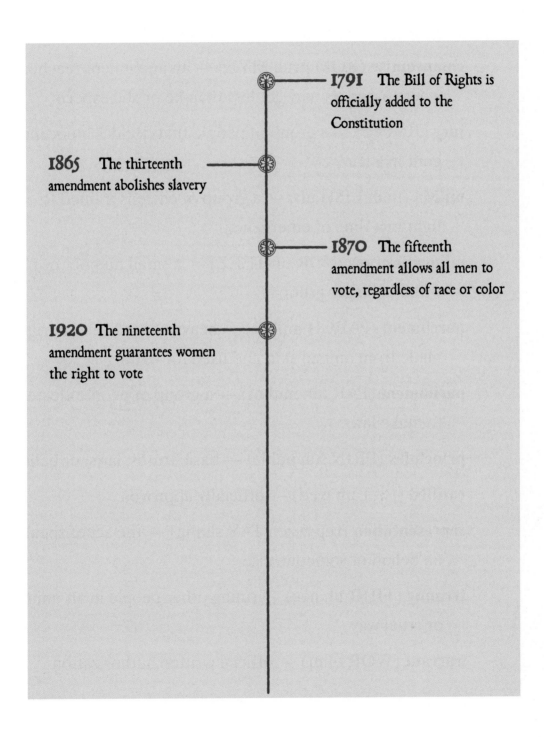

1791 The Bill of Rights is officially added to the Constitution

1865 The thirteenth amendment abolishes slavery

1870 The fifteenth amendment allows all men to vote, regardless of race or color

1920 The nineteenth amendment guarantees women the right to vote

GLOSSARY

adopted (uh DOPT ed) — to formally put into effect

compromise (KOM pruh MYZ) — an agreement reached where a person may get less than he or she expects

jury (JUR ee) — a group of people that decides innocence or guilt in a trial

militia (muh LISH uh) — a group of citizens trained to fight in a time of emergency

minorities (mye NOR uh TEEZ) — a small number or part within a bigger group

parchment (PARCH muhnt) — heavy paper like material made from animal skin and used for writing

parliament (PAR luh muhnt) — a group of people elected to make laws

principles (PRIN suh puhlz) — basic truths, laws, or beliefs

ratified (RAT uh fyed) — officially approved

representation (rep ri zen TAY shuhn) — the act of speaking on behalf of someone else

tyranny (TIHR uh nee) — ruling other people in an unjust or cruel way

warrant (WOR uhnt) — official written authorization

FURTHER READING

Freedman, Russell. *In Defense of Liberty: The Story of America's Bill of Rights.* Holiday House, 2003.

Hudson Jr., David L. *The Bill of Rights: The First Ten Amendments of the Constitution.* Enslow Publishers, Inc., 2002.

Sobel, Syl. *The U.S. Constitution and You.* Barron's Educational Services, Inc. 2001.

WEBSITES TO VISIT

www.archives.gov/national_archives_experience/bill_of_rights.html

www.congressforkids.net/Constitution_index.htm

www.constitutioncenter.org/explore/TheU.S.Constitution/index.shtml

ABOUT THE AUTHORS

David and Patricia Armentrout have written many nonfiction books for young readers. They have had several books published for primary school reading. The Armentrouts live in Cincinnati, Ohio, with their two children.

INDEX

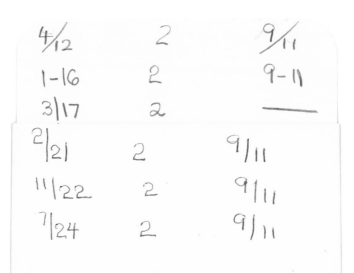

4/12	2	9/11
1-16	2	9-11
3/17	2	—
2/21	2	9/11
11/22	2	9/11
7/24	2	9/11

BAKER & TAYLOR